Bit Coin
Crypto Cash

What is Bit coin?

Bit coin crypto cash can be utilizated to purchase things electronically. It resembles traditional US Dollars, Euros, Japan yen, which are additionally exchanged carefully.

Bit coin's crypto cash most vital trademark, and the thing that makes it diverse to customary cash, is that it is decentralized. No single organization controls the bit coin crypto cash arrange. This comforts a few people, since it implies that a major bank can't control their money.

Bit coin has caught the overall population creative ability in the course of the most recent couple of years. It has made a few people rich, been the objective of cybercrime examinations, and reformed the way that individuals consider money. Numerous legislatures in any case don't no ifs ands or buts comprehend what to do around it. However what is it, precisely?

A system where nobody is in charge

Bit coin is a fresh out of the plastic new state of virtual cash with one vast qualification over the sorts of money that we're utilized to: nobody controls it.

Conventional cash is made by method for critical banks, who conclude that it exists, after which utilize it to look for specialists bonds. Charge systems and banks deal with the way it's moved around, and they charge you liberally for the benefit. They're the watchmen of the money related gadget.

Bit coin changes all that. It's a decentralized value group, wherein no unmarried man or lady or business endeavor controls how money is made or moved around. Or maybe, anybody on the group controls their own cash. Every individual is their own one of a kind guard. Also, completely everybody can take part, by methods for downloading the detached piece coin programming program and walking it all alone PC.

Shouldn't something be said about Misrepresentation?

There should be rules, however, or individuals could dedicate all assortments of misrepresentation. People would potentially send somebody a bit coin and after that say that they hadn't, with the goal that they may spend it somewhere else. That is an inconvenience alluded to as 'twofold spending', and bit coin is intended to avoid it happening.

The majority of the PCs strolling the product program are connected on the whole through the net, and every one of them keep an eye settled on each unique to verify that everybody is betting by method for the arrangements.

This system of PCs is the bit coin expense system, and it's a basic a piece of the total piece coin marvel. Bit coins wouldn't exist in any noteworthy shape without the installment arrange.

The system keeps melody of who is sending bit coins to various people, and what number of bit coins every individual has. In the event that anybody attempted to state that they hadn't spent piece coin when they clearly had, then whatever is left of the group may know.

How Are Bit coins made?

The network is also liable for making bit coins inside the first area. Bit coins aren't published, or dreamed up by using an imperative financial institution. As an alternative, people create bit coins using software on their personal computer systems, in a technique known as mining (learn greater about mining here). The community has guidelines approximately many bit coins are created, who receives to create them, and whilst.

Bit coins Held

Bit coins aren't physical cash, and furthermore you don't store them in a money related organization. They least difficult exist in light of the fact that the whole group agrees that they exist, and you handiest claim them because of the reality the group is of a similar supposition which you do. This record of possession is held in a major record called the square chain that is noticeable and kept up by utilizing the greater part of the PC frameworks at the bit coin group. Analyze additional roughly the piece chain here.

This record proceeds with tune of who claims all the bit coins on the group, be that as it may it doesn't utilize names, or money related organization accounts. Rather, it makes utilization of bit coin addresses that are long strings of arbitrary characters. There's no simple method for knowing who possesses a bit coin address, which makes the framework unknown if utilized effectively.

each time completely everybody sends bit coins to a man else, they advise the system to supplant the record all together that the bit coins are charged from their address, and credited to the inverse manage.

One and all observes that change.

What Do Bit coins appear like?

Nonetheless if bit coins are not substantial money, in what manner will you hold them? You don't. As an option, you hold a report of an open piece coin adapt to, that is a broadened series of numbers and letters. You likewise keep a riddle key (consider it like a secret word) that helps you to utilize that arrangement with to ship bit coins. You could keep that address in a product program pockets, or it might likewise be distributed on a touch of paper.

Keep in mind, the group itself has the records about which addresses keep up which bit coins. All you're putting away is the mystery key that helps you to get admission to the bit coins at a particular address.

That is the sole component giving you ownership of these bit coins.

Transparency

There is one last capacity of the bit coin story: straightforwardness. regardless of the way that handiest the holder of an individual key can get section to the keys at a bit coin manage, anyone can perceive what number of bit coins are held at that arrangement with, which distinctive locations they arrived from, and how they were spent.

Inside the managing an account worldwide, your record is connected for your name, and it's non-open. In the bit coin worldwide, you can track a bit coin's presence from its underlying creation through to the present day, seeing which addresses have spent and gotten it. However your name is not the slightest bit identified with it on the bit coin organize.

Bit coin is an unprecedented blend, then. It's remote cash that is additionally an expense arrange. It's each anonymous (if utilized well) and totally straightforward. It's decentralized, however with rules that are entirely authorized.

Satoshi Nakamoto

Satoshi Nakamoto is the name used by the dark individual or individuals who arranged piece coin and made its exceptional reference utilization, Bit coin Center. As a bit of the execution, they also invented the essential square chain database. In the process they were the first to deal with the twofold spending issue for cutting edge money. They were progressive in the headway of bit coin up until December 2010.

Nakamoto has ensured to do what needs to be done living in Japan, imagined around 1975. Nevertheless, hypothesis about the real character of Nakamoto has generally focused on different cryptography and programming designing pros of non-Japanese dive, living in the Amassed States and Europe. One individual, Australian programming engineer Craig Steven Wright, has stated to be Nakamoto, nonetheless he has not yet offered confirmation of this.

Beginning at 2 February 2017, Nakamoto is acknowledged to have up to around one million piece coins, with a regard evaluated at over US$1.1 billion.

"Satoshi Nakamoto" is set out to be a pseudonym the individual or people who arranged the main piece coin tradition in 2008 and impelled the framework in 2009. Nakamoto was accountable for making the greater part of the expert piece coin programming and was progressive in making adjustments and posting specific information on the BitcoinTalk Discourse.

Examinations concerning the certified identity of Satoshi Nakamoto were tried by The New Yorker and Fast Association. The New Yorker's examination raised no under two possible contenders: Michael Clear and Abominable Lehdonvirta. Brisk Association's examination raised restrictive verification interfacing an encryption patent application recorded by Neal Ruler, Vladimir Kosmas and Charles Brie on 15 August

2008, and the bitcoin.org territory name which was enlisted 72 hours sometime later. The patent application (#20100042841) contained frameworks organization and encryption progressions as coin bit, and scholarly examination revealed that the expression "... computationally irrational to switch" appeared in both the patent application and bit coin's whitepaper. Each one of the three creators unequivocally denied being Satoshi Nakamoto. In May 2013, Ted Nelson evaluated that Japanese mathematician Shinichi Mochizuki is Satoshi Nakamoto. Later in 2013 the Israeli experts Doris Ron and Help Shamir demonstrated Silk Road associated Ross William Ulbricht as the possible individual behind the cover. The two authorities build their uncertainty in light of an examination of the arrangement of bit coin trades. These cases were tested. Ron and Shamir later pulled back their claim.

Nakamoto's consideration with bit coin does not appear to extend past mid-2010. In April 2011, Nakamoto talked with a bit coin supporter, saying that he had "continued ahead to various things".

Stefan Thomas, a Swiss coder and element assemble part, charted the time stamps for each of Nakamoto's at least 500 piece coin discourse posts; the consequent diagram exhibited a grandiose rot to no posts between the hours of 5 a.m. likewise, 11 a.m. Greenwich Mean Time. Since this illustration stayed steady even on Saturdays and Sundays, it prescribed that Nakamoto was dozing starting at now, and the hours of 5 a.m. to 11 a.m. GMT are midnight to 6 a.m. Eastern Standard Time (North American Eastern Standard Time). Distinctive snippets of data suggested that Nakamoto was English: An every day paper include he had encoded at the outset square began from the UK-circulated day by day paper The Conditions, and both his discourse posts and his comments in the bit coin source code used English spellings, for instance, "streamline" and "shading".

An Internet look by an obscure blogger of works tantamount in keeping in touch with the bit coin whitepaper prescribes Scratch Sabot's "bit gold" articles as having a near author. Scratch denied being Satoshi, and communicated his official supposition on Satoshi and bit coin in a May 2011 article.

In a Walk 2014 article in Newsweek, feature writer Leah McGrath Goodman dosed Dorian S. Nakamoto of Asylum City, California, saying that Satoshi Nakamoto is the man's unique name. Her procedures and conclusion drew broad criticism.

In June 2016, the London Study of Books appropriated a piece by Andrew O'Hagan about Nakamoto.

Development bit coin

In October 2008, Nakamoto circulated a paper on The Cryptography Mailing list at metzdowd.com delineating the bit coin mechanized money. It was titled Piece coin: A Dispersed Electronic Cash System. In January 2009, Nakamoto released the vital piece coin programming that moved the framework and the essential units of the bit coin crypto money, called bit coins. Satoshi Nakamoto released the bit coin programming on Source manufacture on 9 January 2009. Version 0.1 was orchestrated using Microsoft Visual Studio.

The maker of bit coin understood that as a result of its disposition the inside arrangement would need the ability to support a far reaching extent of trade sorts. The realized plan enabled particular codes and data fields from the start utilizing a predicative script.

Nakamoto made a site with the space name bitcoin.org and continued cooperating with various architects on the bit coin programming until mid-2010. Around this time, he gave over control of the source code storage facility and framework prepared key to Gavin Andresen, traded a couple related territories to various discernible people from the bit coin aggregate, and ended his relationship in the wander. Until right away before his nonappearance and handover,

Nakamoto rolled out all improvements to the source code themselves.

The maker left a text in the at first mined square which examines 'The Conditions 03/Jan/2009 Chancellor on skirt of second bailout for banks'. The substance suggests a component in The Conditions conveyed on 3 January 2009. It is a strong sign that the central square was mined no sooner than this date. The starting piece has a timestamp of 18:15:05 GMT on January 3 2009. This piece is not under any condition like each and every other square in that it doesn't have past square to reference. This

Required the usage of custom code to mine it. Timestamps for coming about pieces demonstrate that Nakamoto did not endeavor to mine all the early squares only for themselves with a true objective to benefit by a pansy plot.

As the sole, win early digger the maker was conceded bit coin at starting and for 10 days a short time later. Beside test trades these stay unspent since mid January 2009. General society bit coin trade log exhibits that Nakamoto's known areas contain around one million piece coins. Beginning at 7 February 2017, this is the thing that should be brought over US$1 billion.

Attributes

Nakamoto did not uncover any individual information while looking at specific matters. They gave some evaluate on dealing with a record and incomplete hold crediting. On his P2P Foundation profile beginning at 2012, Nakamoto attested to be a 37-year-old male who lived in Japan, yet some estimated he was most likely not going to be Japanese in light of his usage of flawless English and his bit coin programming not being accounted for or named in Japanese.

Occasional English spelling and wording, (for instance, the expression "underhanded hard") in both source code comments and discourse postings provoked hypothesis that Nakamoto, or if nothing else one individual in the consortium ensuring to be him, was of Ward cause.

Stefan Thomas, a Swiss coder and element assemble part, charted the time stamps for each of Nakamoto's bit coin gathering posts (more than 500); the ensuing diagram showed an unsafe rot to no posts between the hours of 5 a.m. in addition, 11 a.m. Greenwich Mean Time. Since this case stayed steady even on Saturdays and Sundays, it recommended that Nakamoto was napping starting at now. If Nakamoto is a single individual with standard resting affinities, it suggests he stayed in a zone using the UTC–05:00 or UTC–06:00 time adjust. This joins the parts of North

America that fall inside the Eastern Time Zone and Central Time Zone, and also parts of Central America, the Caribbean and South America.

Gavin Andresen has said of Nakamoto's code "He was an astonishing coder, notwithstanding it was unconventional".

Applicants

There is still instability about the real character of Satoshi Nakamoto.

Nick Szabo

In December 2013, a blogger named Skye Dim associated Scratch Szabo to the bit coin whitepaper using a stylometric examination. Szabo is a decentralized money darling and circulated a paper on "bit gold", which is seen as a precursor to bit coin. He is known to have been possessed with using assumed names the 1990s. In a May 2011 article, Szabo communicated about the bit coin creator: "Myself, Wei Dai, and Hal Finney were the fundamental people I am mindful of who adored the idea (or for Dai's circumstance his related thought) enough to look for after it to any basic degree until Nakamoto (tolerating Nakamoto is not by any extend of the creative ability Finney or Dai)."

Natty coarse research by cash related maker Dominic Frisbee gives much coincidental affirmation in any case, as he yields, no confirmation that Satoshi is Szabo. Chatting on RT's The Keiser Report, he said "I've completed up there is only a solitary individual in the whole world that has the sheer broadness also the specificity of data and it is this chap ..." Yet, Szabo has denied being Satoshi. In a July 2014 email to Frisbee, he expressed: 'Thankful for letting me know. I'm confounded you overlooked what's really important doing me as Satoshi, yet I'm used to it'. Nathaniel Popper wrote in the New York Times that "the most inducing verification demonstrated a separated American man of Hungarian drop named Scratch Szabo."

Dorian Nakamoto

In December 2013, a blogger named Skye Dull associated Scratch Szabo to the bit coin whitepaper using a stylometric examination. Szabo is a decentralized money partner and disseminated a paper on "bit gold", which is seen as a precursor to bit coin. He is known to have been involved with using pen names the 1990s. In a May 2011 article, Szabo communicated about the bit coin producer: "Myself, Wei Dai, and Hal Finney were the fundamental people I am mindful of who favored the idea (or for Dai's circumstance his related thought) enough to look for after it to any gigantic degree until Nakamoto (expecting Nakamoto is not by any methods Finney or Dai)."

Point by point examine by money related maker Dominic Frisbee gives much contingent affirmation notwithstanding, as he yields, no confirmation that Satoshi is Szabo. Chatting on RT's The Keiser Report, he said "I've shut there is only a solitary individual in the whole world that has the sheer broadness moreover the specificity of data and it is this chap ..." Regardless, Szabo has denied being Satoshi. In a July 2014 email to Frisbee, he expressed: 'An obligation of appreciation is all together to tell me. I'm on edge you overlooked what's really important doing me as Satoshi, be that as it may I'm used to it'. Nathaniel Popper wrote in the New York Times that "the most influencing confirmation demonstrated a withdrawn American man of Hungarian drop named Scratch Szabo."

Dorian Nakamoto

The article's generation incited a tornado of media energy, including reporters outside close Dorian Nakamoto's home and rapidly seeking after him through auto when he made a beeline for a meeting. Regardless, in the midst of the subsequent full-length chat with, Dorian Nakamoto denied all relationship with bit coin, saying he had never known in regards to the money, and that he had misinterpreted Goodman's question as being about his past work for military authoritative laborers, a considerable amount of which was characterized. In a reedit AMA, he stated he'd confused Goodman's question as being related to his work for Citibank. Before long, the pseudonymous Nakamoto's P2P Foundation account posted its first message in five years, communicating: "I am not Dorian Nakamoto."

Hal Finney

Hal Finney (May 4, 1956 – August 28, 2014) was a pre-bit coin cryptographic pioneer and the principle individual (other than Satoshi himself) to use the item, record bug reports, and roll out improvements. He moreover carried on a couple blocks from Dorian Nakamoto's family home, according to Forbes editorialist Andy Greenberg. Greenberg asked the arrangement examination consultancy Joule and Accomplices to differentiate an example of Finney's composed work with Satoshi Nakamoto's and they found that it was the closest resemblance they had yet gone over (checking the contenders proposed by Newsweek, Speedy Association, The New Yorker, Ted Nelson and Skye Dim). Greenberg guessed that Finney may have been an expert author for the advantage of Nakamoto, or that he essentially used his neighbor Dorian's lifestyle as a "drop" or "patsy whose individual information is used to stow away online attempts". In any case, in the wake of meeting Finney, seeing the messages among him and Satoshi, his bit coin wallet's history including the essential piece coin trade (from Satoshi to him, which he fail to pay back) and hearing his repudiation, Greenberg completed

Finney was telling the truth. Joule and Accomplices furthermore found that Satoshi's messages to Finney more almost resemble Satoshi's diverse structures than Finney's do. Finney's related coercion and all over co-blogger Robin Hanson doled out a subjective probability of "no under" 15% that "Hal was more required than he's said", before extra affirmation prescribed that was not the circumstance.

Regulatory

On 18 Walk 2013, the Cash related Wrongdoings Endorsement System (or Finsen), an association of the Gathered States Bureau of the Treasury, issued a report regarding joined together and decentralized "virtual financial measures" and their true blue status inside "cash associations business" (MSB) and Bank Question Act controls. It asked for computerized budgetary rules and other impelled part frameworks, for example, bit coin as "virtual cash related benchmarks" since they are not honest to goodness delicate under any sovereign area. Finsen cleared American clients of bit mint piece of lawful obligations by saying, "A client of virtual cash is not a MSB under Finsen's controls and along these lines is not subject to MSB selection, announcing, and recordkeeping headings." Notwithstanding, it held that American substances who convey "virtual money, for example, bit currencies are cash transmitters or MSBs on the off chance that they offer their conveyed cash for national money: "...a individual that makes units of convertible virtual cash and pitches those units to someone else for legitimate cash or its comparing is had with transmission to another domain and is a cash transmitter." This particularly contacts "excavators" of the bit mint piece money who may need to enlist as MSBs and submit to the good 'ol fashioned basics of being a cash transmitter in the event that they offer their made piece mint pieces for national cash and are inside the Gathered States. Since Finsen issued this course, various virtual money exchangers and officials have selected with Finsen, and Finsen is getting an amplifying number of suspicious improvement reports (SARs) from these substances.

Also, Finsen guaranteed control over American segments that regulate bit coins in a part processor setting or as a trade: "in like way, a man is an exchanger and a cash transmitter if the individual perceives such de-bound together convertible virtual money starting with one individual and transmits it then onto the accompanying individual as a component of the attestation and exchange of cash, assets, or other respect that substitutes for money."

In diagram, Finsen's choice would require bit coin trades where bit coins are exchanged for conventional monetary benchmarks to uncover noteworthy exchanges and suspicious advancement, fit in with assessment evasion controls, and gather data about their clients as standard money related establishments are required to do.

Patrick Merck of the Bit coin Establishment reprimanded Finsen's report as an "outperform" and expressed that Finsen "can't depend on upon this bearing in any utilization activity".

Jennifer Insecure Calvary, the head of Finsen communicated, "Virtual cash related models are committed to an ill defined guidelines from different financial structures. ... Essential cash associations business rules apply here."

In its October 2012 overview, Virtual cash arranges, the European National Bank considered that the progression of virtual monetary rules will proceed, and, given the financial models' trademark regard instability, nonattendance of close bearing, and risk of unlawful uses by darken clients, the Bank educated that accidental examination concerning updates would be crucial to reassess hazards.

In 2013, the U.S. Treasury extended its antagonistic to unlawful obligation avoidance controls to processors of bit coin exchanges.

In June 2013, Piece coin Establishment board part Jon Matonis wrote in Forbes that he got a notice letter from the California Organization of Monetary Affiliations reproaching the establishment for unlicensed cash transmission. Martinis denied that the establishment is had with cash transmission and said he saw the case as "a chance to show state controllers."

In late July 2013, the industry add up to Board for the Foundation of the Modernized Resource Exchange Master started to packaging to set prescribed procedures and measures, to work with controllers and policymakers to modify existing money necessities to bleeding edge cash headway and courses of action of action and make danger association rules.

In 2014, the U.S. Securities and Trade Commission recorded an authoritative development against Erik T. Voorhees, for hurting Securities Act Segment 5 for straightforwardly offering unregistered interests in good for nothing coin goals as a side effect of bit coins.

Theft and exchange

Thievery of bit coin has been accounted for on different occasions. At various conditions, bit coin exchanges have shut down, carrying their clients' bit coins with them. A Wired audit circulated April 2013 exhibited that 45 percent of bit coin exchanges end up closing.

On 19 June 2011, a security break of the Mt. Go bit coin exchange made the apparent cost of a bit coin to misleadingly drop to one penny on the Mt. Go exchange, after a software engineer used capabilities from a Mt. Go analysts exchanged off PC illegally to trade a broad number of bit coins to him. They used the exchange's item to offer them all apparently, making a colossal "ask" mastermind at any cost. Inside minutes, the esteem came back to its correct customer traded regard. Accounts with what should be called more than US$8,750,000 were affected.

In July 2011, the head of Biomet, the third-greatest piece coin exchange, detailed that he had lost access to his wallet.dat archive with around 17,000 piece coins (by and large equivalent to US$220,000 around then). He detailed that he would offer the organization for the missing aggregate, intending to use saves from the arrangement to markdown his customers.

In August 2011, MyBitcoin, a now obsolete piece coin trade processor, declared that it was hacked, which made it be shut down, paying 49% on customer stores, leaving more than 78,000 piece coins (corresponding to by and large US$800,000 around then) unaccounted for.

At the start of August 2012, a case was archived in San Francisco court against Bitcoinica — a bit coin trading scene — declaring about US$460,000 from the association. Bitcoinica was hacked twice in 2012, which incited claims that the scene ignored the security of customers' money and cheated them out of withdrawal requesting.

In late August 2012, an operation titled Piece coin Hold finances and Trust was shut around the proprietor, leaving around US$5.6 million in bit coin-based commitments; this incited charges that the operation was a Penza contrive. In September 2012, the U.S. Securities and Exchange Commission had clearly started an examination investigating the issue.

In September 2012, Piece floor, a bit coin exchange, in like manner reported being hacked, with 24,000 piece coins (worth about US$250,000) stolen. Along these lines, Bit floor suspended operations. That month, Bit floor proceeded with operations; its creator said that he uncovered the theft to FBI, and that he needs to repay the setbacks, however the time traverse for repayment is dim.

On 3 April 2013, Instawallet, an online wallet provider, was hacked, realizing the burglary of more than 35,000 piece coins which were regarded at US$129.90 per bit coin at the time, or practically $4.6 million by and large. Therefore, Instawallet suspended operations.

On 11 August 2013, the Bit coin Foundation pronounced that a bug in a pseudorandom number generator inside the Android working structure had been abused to take from wallets delivered by Android applications; fixes were given 13 August 2013.

In October 2013, Inputs.io, an Australian-based piece coin wallet provider was hacked with lost 4100 piece coins, worth over a$1 million at time of theft. The organization was controlled by the executive Exchange Post. Coin visit, the related piece coin talk room, has been expected control by another head.

On 26 October 2013, a Hong-Kong based piece coin trading stage asserted by Overall Bond Obliged (GBL) vanished with 30 million Yuan (US$5 million) from 500 monetary pros.

Mt. Go, the Japan-based exchange that in 2013 managed 70% of all general piece coin development, defaulted on a few advances in February 2014, with bit coins worth about $390 million missing, for dim reasons. The President was over the long haul caught and blamed for misappropriation.

On 3 Walk 2014, Flex coin proclaimed it was closing its portals accordingly of a hack attack that happened the day going before. In a declaration that now includes their point of arrival, they wrote about 3 Walk 2014 that "As Flex coin does not have the benefits, assets, or by and large to come back from this setback [the hack], we are closing our gateways rapidly." Customers can no longer sign into the site.

Chinese crypto money exchange Biter lost $2.1 million in BTC in February 2015.

The Slovenian exchange Bit stamp lost piece coin worth $5.1 million to a hack in January 2015.

The US-construct exchange Sepulchers defaulted with respect to a few credits in January 2016, evidently by virtue of a 2014 hacking event; the court-assigned recipient later charged that Tombs' Leader had stolen $3.3 million.

In May 2016, Entryway Coin close quickly after a crack had achieved lost about $2 million in crypto money. It pledged to restore and reimburse its customers.

In August 2016, software engineers stole some $72 million in customer bit coin from the Hong-Kong-based exchange Bitfinex.

Predictions

Bit coin's crypto money history was ideal. Expected of bit coin crypto cash (2019) 1 bit coin crypto money proportionate $1800 - $2500 USD.

ISBN 9781985009103